Philosophical
Poems

Savage

PRESS

Superior, WI

Other Books by E. M. Johnson

Gleanings From the Hillsides

Poems of Faith and Inspiration

Philosophical
Poems

A Philosophy from a Different Viewpoint

By E.M. Johnson

First Edition

Printed in 1999

© Copyright 1999 Elizabeth Coon

Cover Illustration and all artwork ©1999 Miriam Wilms

ISBN 1-886028-41-9

Library of Congress Catalog Card Number: 99-071243

Published by:
Savage Press
P.O. Box 115, Superior, WI 54880
715-394-9513

e-mail: savpress@spacestar.com

Visit us at: www.savpress.com

Printed in the USA

Acknowledgments

Thanks to:
Dorothy Johnson
Eugene Coon
Miriam Wilms
Elizabeth Coon
Mike Savage
Hugo Wilms
David and Julie Coon.

Preface

Edwin M. Johnson was born May 20, 1891, in Eau Claire, Wisconsin. His parents were born in Norway and immigrated to the U.S.A. He lived in Owen, Wisconsin from the age of two to sixteen and attended Northland College in Ashland, Wisconsin from 1907 to 1913. He later graduated from Superior State Teachers College and taught in various northern Wisconsin high schools beside being a principal for twenty-two years. An interesting feature of his life was that he worked in the sawmill in Owen, at the age of twelve, loading "short" lumber on Saturdays in the summer.

The late John Chapple of the Ashland Daily Press wrote the following of Mr. Johnson: "During my more than 60-years of active association with the Daily Press, this is the fourth time the writing of a real poet has emerged to the best of my recollections. The other three were Dr. Kate Kelsey-Clark of Cable, Wisconsin, the late Joe Moran of Glidden, Wisconsin and the late Reverend James Sanaker of Ashland, Wisconsin. They all wrote lovingly of the north country —not only lovingly, but with rare technical ability that ranks their writing as real poetry. The late Edwin Johnson is one of this quartet of great poets in our history.

"Much of his poetry sings with beauty. It is uplifiting. It makes life more worthwhile just to read it. Mr. Johnson breathed his love of our area into pearls of beauty."

Mr. Johnson's wife, the late Dorothy Horn Johnson, wrote these words about her husband: "I have been faced with the task of selecting a representative group from the hundreds of poems that Edwin struck off at the slightest provocation, (She had a small volume of his poems published for family and friends.) His hobbies were fishing, hunting and rhyming. The latter kept him occupied after he had been forced through ill health to forego the others. Often while outdriving he would be seized with an idea for a poem saying, 'Give me my pencil and pad. I must get down the thought that just flew by.' He often sat transfixed in church as the seed of a thought took root, possibly from the sermon, hastening home to write it down before it escaped him.

"Living in the north woods of Wisconsin the greater share of his life, he was closely attuned to nature in all its forms. Flowers and birds, trees and animals became a life study, and his spirit responded to every phase of the natural world. Of a religious nature as well, he attempted to express the relationship of God and man, the unity of all of God's creation, and the mystery of the universe as far as it was possible for him to do so. In short, he was a philosopher of sorts."

Edwin M. Johnson died in Ashland, Wisconsin in July 1968. His appreciation for God's handiwork lives on through his poetry

Log home in Delta, Wisconsin where Mr. Johnson
wrote much of his poetry.

Dedication

This book is dedicated in very loving memory to Miriam Johnson Wilms, daughter of Edwin M. Johnson. She passed away January 17th, 1997. Miriam was the artist who did all the illustrations for this and the other two E.M. Johnson books.

Foreword

The poems in this book have come to me largely from my contact with the out of doors. They are thoughts expressed by others in many ways far better. Yet because the heredity and environment of each makes an entity unto itself, it is possible that these lines may bring forth a philosophy from a different viewpoint.

There is a pattern in life, of this I am convinced. There is a rhythm of creation, the overtones of which, are all about us. There is a oneness, in all creation and man is but a part of that great mosaic which time weaves on the Loom of the Universe. The Part is in the Whole and the Whole is in the Part, and God is man's ultimate goal.

The thoughts I herein have set to verse I realize full well are but scattered fragments of Truth shattered in places by the dischords of halting meter. I can but trust that some of these fragments may pattern in part at least the philosophy of my readers. If any bit of rhythm, any picture projected or any thoughts of mine bring comfort, "When the sun is hid 'neath a cloud," I shall be glad.

Without hope, the soul of man atrophies. May the following verses bring some small ray of light through the darkness of despair and defeat that comes sometimes, to us all.

> If I have written some bit of song,
> That has eased some brother's pain,
> Or cheered one heart, dispelled one fear,
> I have not written in vain.
>
> I'll thank The Lord, for that one verse,
> For even one short line;
> I'll lay not claim to any theme,
> Each thought, Oh Lord, is Thine.

— EMJ

Table of Contents

Culmination 13
Just a Smile 14
The Golden Thread 15
Ideals 17
Thought is the Metal 18
The Thoughts that we Think 19
As the Dial is Set 21
Thoughts of God 22
The Crags of Thought 23
An Arc of Thought 24
The Pattern of Thought 26
From Thought to Energy 27
Thought is Reality I 27
Thought is Reality II 29
An Early Morning Thought 30
A Thought for the Day 31
A Thought for the Day 32
Too much and too Fast 33
Inscribed in the Hearts of All 34
Regrets 36
The Rendevous I 37
The Rendevous II 38
Life's Bluff 39
Mariners 40
The Spectrum 41
The Full Circle of Truth 42
Brew from the Caludron of Hell 43
Worries, Stress and Strain 44
Riches 45
Tempered Steel 46
Projection into the Country Beyond 47
Shoddy Cloth or a Garment of Gold? 48
How did you meet Defeat? 49
The Loom 50
Harmonic 52

Table of Contents

An Ancient Wisdom 53
The Mystery 54
Then Cherish Beauty 56
From Dawn Unto Darkness 57
Polarization 58
Lightly Time Steals O'er the Heart 59
Beyond Recall 60
These Alone Can Man Possess 61
The Fourth Dimension 62
Treasure Beyond Measure 63
Contentment 64
The Quest 67
High Though the Heavens 68
A Bit of Contrast 69
Cause and Effect 70
Full Runs the Spring 71
Liberalism 72
An Ancient Law 74
What did He Bring Back Home? 75
Nature Abhors a Vacuum 76
Continuity 77
Universality 78
Giants of the Earth 79
Greater Than Thebes or Rome 80
Sands on the Sea Shore 82
Higher Than Creed 84
Kinship 85
Could it be Something Intangible 86
Riding the Storm 87
A Path Across a Hill 88
Forever Cycling 90
Chinks in the Wall 91
The Gleam 92
So Little, Yet so Great 93

Table of Contents

Mister Big 96
Three Men and a Mountain 98
Linnaea Borealis 99
The Body, the Mind, the Soul 100
Come on Fairy Wings 101
Epilogue 102

Culmination

The past, no matter what it be
Is like the breeze that stirs the sea;
You cannot change the wind's wide sweep
Nor alter the past—why mourn and weep?

The future with its winsome ways
And all the allure that it displays
Lies always just beyond the hill
Which scaled, reveals one farther still.

Only the present is yours to hold.
To shape, to fold, to press and mold;
In the present lie the why and when
Of all that shall be, or ever has been.

E. M. Johnson

Just A Smile

How little it takes to make life happy,
Oh, so little to make life glad;
But it takes no more than this,
Just as little to make life sad.

Just a smile brings back the sunshine,
Drives the cheerless clouds away,
While a frown or thoughtless word
Steals the brightness from the day.

Just some trifle we've omitted
In our greed to grasp at things;
Lo, before we e'en have clutched them,
Love and joy have taken wings.

So very little to make life happy,
E'en less than this to make life sad.
But a smile will bring the sunshine
Back to hearts and make them glad.

The Golden Thread

There's a golden thread of the brightest hue,
Spun through the hearts of men.
Its color is more rare than the delicate blue
Of the flower that grows in the fen.
For it's made of the strands of the stars that shine,
A part of the soul of God,
And He spun it fine, when he made man divine,
And raised him up from the sod.

But the thread grows twisted and warped and sear,
The pattern fades in the light,
Whenever we fail, from greed or fear
To do that which is noble and right.
But kindness and thought for others care,
We give on Life's road, each day,
Will burnish the gold and mend every tear,
That selfishness dims, dull gray.

Each thought that we think, each act that we do,
Be it noble and just, or wrong,
Will tarnish the strands, or brighten the hue,
Will weaken or make them strong.
For each life is a part of a pattern, dull gray,
Or the warp of a noble design,
And the things that we do, the thoughts of each day,
Mar that pattern, or make it divine.

E. M. Johnson

Ideals

As you think, you travel; and as you love,
    you attract.
You are today where your thoughts have
    brought you;
You will be tomorrow where your thoughts
    take you.
You cannot escape the results of your
    thoughts,
But you can endure and learn, and accept
    and be glad.
You will realize the vision (not the idle
    wish) of your heart,
Be it base or beautiful, or a mixture of
    both,
For you will always gravitate towards that
    which you secretly, most love.
In your hands will be placed the exact
    results of your thoughts;
You will receive that which you earn;
    no more, no less.
What ever your present environment may be,
    you will fall,
Remain, or rise with your thoughts, your
    wisdom, your IDEAL.

E. M. Johnson

Thought is the Metal

It is said, by our acts we shall be known;
    full well this may be true.
But this I've also learned from Life;
    no matter what we do,
Whatever we seek to accomplish;
    whate'er in Life is wrought,
It is on the Anvil of the Mind,
    we hammer deeds from Thought.

Thought, is the metal, pliable, malleable,
    from which each Deed is made;
Thought is the metal from which is carved
    each Deed like the tempered blade.
Thought is the metal God gives to each
    on which a Life to engrave.
And the Thoughts we think, are the Deeds we carve
    that make us Free Men or Slave.

"By our acts," 'tis said, we shall be known."
    we are judged by what we do.
But this much I've learned as well in Life,
    and this much I know to be true;
Whatever in life of good or ill,
    we've hammered from our thought;
For the mind is the forge that tempers the steel
    from which each Life is wrought.

Philosophical Poems

The Thoughts that we Think

If waves of sound roll on forever
Through endless boundless space,
And beams of light speed on forever
In their endless streaming race,
Then surely Thought, life's motivation
Rolls onward wave upon wave,
And leaves its imprint on all creation
From birth and unto the grave.

Around us they whirl, forever winging,
Thoughts form the Mind of God.
All nature responds in symphonies ringing
From bush from flower and sod.
And man responds when the breath divine,
Gently stirs the heart strings.
And then in unison with the stars they shine
His thought in harmony he brings.

In these moments diving he catches God's thought
Though blurred and dim it be.
And he glimpses in part how worlds are wrought
And the wonders of earth and sea.
He visions in part he can ne'er see the Whole
He hears but fragments harmonic.
Yet ever around us God's music doth roll
In vibrating chords symphonic.

And God gave each mind this power to shine
To send forth rays of thought.
For whatever we think, be it false, or divine

E. M. Johnson

In some heart the deeds will be wrought.
Some imprint we make on the lives of others
By all that we think and do,
But more than all, tis the thought from mothers
that help us to be kind and true.

Yes waves of sound roll on forever,
Through boundless endless space.
And beams of light speed on forever
In an endless streaming race.
And stamped on all, throughout creation
From birth and beyond the grave,
Every thought we think, in its motivation,
Rolls onward, wave upon wave.

Philosophical Poems

As the Dial is Set

No thoughts were ever created by men,
Though voiced by mouth, by print or pen.
All thoughts of good, or truth or love,
Come direct from the Mind of God above.
All thoughts of evil, from Hell are spewed,
And the devil has many a foul brood.

Now men of science, may well disagree,
But this is the way it looks to me:
The mind of man is a receiving set,
According to the dial, are the thoughts he will get.
We change the wave at our own free will,
To pick up thoughts of good or of ill.

For man does not build, he but imitates
All that God, through the ages creates.
Whatever is shaped by the hand of man,
You'll find the pattern in God's own plan.
Man does not create, no matter what he's wrought,
His mind, a receiving set, for the wave lengths of
thought.

E. M. Johnson

Thoughts of God

When I behold a tree or shrub,
Or a dawn-tinted orchid flower,
A slow-storm raging o'er the hills,
Of the dance of a summer shower,
And gaze in awe at the countless ships,
In that rim-less sea on high,
Whose guiding lights were trimmed by time,
And hung across the sky—
In each of these, how clear I see,
A completed thought of divinity!

Not one detail left incomplete,
Not one thing left undone.
One thought a flower and one a shower,
An earth, or a blazing sun!

The Crags of Thought

All through the ages Man has climbed
As the secrets of God he's sought
Scaling the heights through dim and obscure,
Climbing the crags of Thought.

When he reaches an apparent summit
Broad vistas turn and twist
And endless beyond, rise crag upon crag
Shrouded in fog and mist.

Endless, forever the search progresses—
The boundaries of Truth diverge.
Crag upon crag, they urge man onward,
But the boundaries of mind converge.

Though dimly and darkly the mind perceives
The wonders God has wrought
Still must we climb, step by step
The endless crags of Thought.

E. M. Johnson

An Arc of Thought

If I could think one thought, compete
In its entirety,
Why then, I know, I'd grasp that, which
Is life's reality.

For every thought is a pattern whole,
Out from a cloth pure white;
Or torn from a shoddy fabric, frayed
And dyed in the vat of night.

The fullness of wisdom, a man's distant goal,
It seems must surely be,
When he can circumscribe and bound
Each thought's entirety.

"We see in part," said a Seer of old,
"Through a glass we see," but an arc.
Yet the boundaries of thought, though ever near,
Lie beyond, in a fringe that's dark.

It's true, I know, God gives to some
The gift and power to see,
More detail and farther around,
Each thought's immensity.

Be this my prayer, from day to day:
"God, Thou who are the Light,
Shine through the fog of self, that
May guide me, through the night.

Philosophical Poems

"In more detail and farther out,
Oh, God, extend the arc,
That I may see, one thought complete,
Whose boundaries, Lord, are dark!"

E. M. Johnson

The Pattern of Thought

A thought sped by on silent wing,
It's shadow fled along.
I grasped for it with eager hands
To pattern it in song.

But I tore its flimsy edges;
Its strands of silken lace
Slipped through my clumsy fingers
And drifted into space.

I tried in vain to shape again
Those wings of heaven-blue,
But who save God can shape at morn
The blossom pearled with dew?

The thought was gone! I had but shreds
Of that which God had wrought;
Yet in my heart there lingers now
The shadow of His thought.

Philosophical Poems

From Thought to Energy

Above and controlling the laws of nature,
Are spirit forces divine.
Superimposed and intermeshed, and
Around all matter entwine.
These forces are set in motion by thought,
Thought waves propelled from God,
By which He creates and shapes and makes,
Stardust into man or sod.

From thought to energy to matter,
Galaxies, planets or man.
Eternally, the cycles run their course,
As they have since time began.
Outward and onward forever,
The limitless galaxies expand,
How or why, or when or where,
We'll never on Earth, understand.

But try man must or he will rust,
Corrode, and crumble to clay.
Yes, man must vainly seek all truth
Until time shall have passed away.
Each grain he gathers on the endless shore,
From the sands of the shimmering sea,
Shall bring him closer unto his God.
And his own divinity.

E. M. Johnson

Thought is Reality I

Evil is born in the depths of the mind,
No matter how it is wrought.
And every wrong that's committed by man,
Was first committed in thought.

And every attribute of goodness,
Like a flower hidden in a seed,
Grows from the germ of a thought,
To unfold in some worthy deed.

For thought is the ultimate reality,
It was thought created space,
Redirecting the channels of a nation's thought,
Dictators enslave an entire race.

"As a man thinketh," it once was said,
When on earth a Master taught,
For out of the heart flows good or ill,
From the endless rivers of thought.

Thought is Reality II

This truth I know was taught by sages
Far in the dim and misty ages.
It is part and parcel of every creed,
Forgotten by many, while few take heed;
And the truth is this:

Each act we do, of good or ill,
Whatever deed we've wrought,
Is but the outward expression and
Completeness of that deed's thought.
Far less tangible is the act
Whose outer form we see;
For unto God, who sees the heart,
Thought is reality.

E. M. Johnson

An Early Morning Thought

Thus life, oft death, gravitates
and grows concentric from, one
little detail, that in our hurry to
achieve the ultimate, we so often
over look. There is a chain of events,
the linking of which is life, and each
thought, each little act, the links that
constitute the same. Life gravitates
from the center of the details of each
day, the minutest constituting, the
ultimate Reality.

Philosophical Poems

A Thought for the Day

Evil attracts evil just as good draws to itself the good around us. This is an irrefutable moral law as unchangeable as the physical laws of gravitation. Evil builds its own concentric accretions which eventually darkens the chamber of the heart shutting out the last rays of hope for God intended development of complete manhood or womanhood.

Good builds itself in ever widening circles until the sunshine of truth overflows the heart and floods the life with hope.

November 11, 1958

A Thought for the Day

Though most of us fail to recognize it and many of us refuse to acknowledge it, we do never the less, live in and are surrounded by a plasma of spirit whose rhythmic waves constantly beat upon our consciousness day and night. There are brief intervals when many of us catch these spirit impulses. A few souls are ever aware of their impact, and alas, there are those lives so discordant that they have grown insensible to all resonance that emanates from the Source of Creation.

It was for the retuning of lives damped by evil that The Great Musician of Galilee came to earth, heralded by a chorus echoed around the world. There can be no true joy, no enduring happiness in our lives unless we are in tune with this Eternal Symphony.

November 25, 1958

E. M. Johnson

A Thought for the Day

Few men are long remembered for the material success they may have achieved in life. But none are ever forgotten for the kindness and understanding they may have shown to a friend, to foe, or stranger.

The attributes of God himself are hereby revealed through the simplest of these acts. Each bit of kindness, whatever the degree, may without our knowledge, cast some ray of sunshine across the dark pathway of some lone fellow traveler.

A Thought for the Day

No man has earned the reward of a better life in a better world beyond this life who has not laid the foundation for that better life, day by day through some small act of kindness and consideration for his fellow man.

As it was said of old, "Even a cup of water given in my name," will be recorded in letters of gold in the book of judgement. So little it takes and yet so much it makes in the total credits of the final accounting of our lives.

Philosophical Poems

Too Much and Too Fast

Today we ride when we used to walk,
We look and listen when we used to talk,
We're too concerned with material things,
With bubbles that burst, and dreams without wings—
Where is the heart that lifts and sings?

We drive through the park,
We don't hear the lark
That sings while he wings on high;
When the day is done and the crimsoned sun
Sings low in the western sky.

So seldom we heed as the shadows steal
That reverence of heart we so seldom feel.
For we lost our way when we forgot to pray
And rend our thanks for the joys of the day.

Too much, too fast, too thoughtless!
Dulled by the day's empty care,
Blind to the beauty around us
And the goodness of God everywhere.

E. M. Johnson

Inscribed in the Hearts of All

One set out, to seek fame and renown,
His ego, you see, was great.
He'd climb to the top, not matter what
Was in store for him, by fate.
So he pushed his way and climbed every day
One rung on the ladder of fame,
He rode rough-shod over man, over God,
And made his own rules of the game.

Yes, he climbed his way to the ladder's top,
For his was the Midas touch.
And great was his name and greater his fame,
Among those, where success means so much.
Yet he came to the end as all men do,
And large was the stone on his grave.
But small was it all in the Judgement Hall,
As small as the little he gave.

And one there was with talents few,
With a background of humble birth,
He toiled with his hands and tilled his good lands,
For he loved the feel of the earth.
Nor renown or fame was attached to his name,
But to all, spite the color or creed,
Though little to spare, he always would share,
If a neighbor was ever in need.

Yes, his talents were few, but all of us knew,
This man of the soil pleased God.
For he loved all men, the earth and the stars,

And the smell of fresh-turned sod.
The end came at last, as come it must—
Though small on his grave was the stone,
How large it loomed, deep in our hearts,
When we thought of the kindness he'd shown.

I know if I enter the Judgement Hall,
That knows not renown nor fame,
I'll find there this man who loved the good earth,
And who lived by the rules of the game.
Though little he had, much did he give,
For the great is ever the small,
And that is the reason this man of the soil,
Is inscribed in the hearts of us all.

E. M. Johnson

Regrets

On why must we wait till the morning sun
Or the morrow that never may be
To speak the kind word, do the kindly deed
That will brighten each memory?

Tho life is so brief and death be so long
Yet we discord so many a note.
When just a kind smile or the kind spoken word
Would bring heaven to earth less remote.

So little it takes to brighten some heart
And to shift some brother's load
Yet somehow too oft we seem to forget
Our neighbor on life's rough road.

Tomorrow we think in our blind simple way
We'll remember to write that letter
Or call on the family by grief so o'erwhelmed
Yet we wait for some day that seems better.

Yes tomorrow, Tomorrow—ah word of regrets
That cuts to the heart like a sword
For Tomorrow I've learned by the man was begot
While Today was made by the Lord.

Then why should we wait until the morning's sun
Oh why must we all wait for Tomorrow?
Tis the unspoken word, the deed left undone
Brings each heart its bitterest sorrow.

The Rendezvous I

There's hush, then a rush of the winds
As they sweep through the tall pine trees,
And I hear in the birch by the stream
The quiver and shiver of leaves.

The grasses bend and the wild winds wend
Their endless, ceaseless way,
And the dark clouds scud, as I hear the thud
Of the surge of the sea, in the bay.

There's a boat that's tossed like a soul that's lost
In the dark, cold currents of life.
While the winds sweep here and then rush there,
In the twisting, turbulent strife.

Quivering, shivering, rushing, hushing,
Lulling the nestling asleep.
Now swift, now slow, they sweep, they flow
Toward a secret space in the deep.

Oft times in the hush and the stillness,
As the westering sun sank slow,
I have heard the call to follow the winds
Follow, wherever they go.

Then a wisp of the winds would whisper
In a cadence tender and true,
"None save the Master of wind and wave
Knoweth our rendezvous."

E. M. Johnson

The Rendezvous II

I called to the wind
But it would not stay.
For it lisped to me
As it sped on it's way
"Do you not see
We cannot delay,
For we have a rendezvous
With the break of day?"

So the wind swept on,
O'er the mountain wall
Not heeding my cry,
Yet I heard it sigh—
"Love comes but once
And when it draws nigh
Grasp it and clasp it
E'er it passes you by."

Life's Bluff

These are the paths that lead out
From every rebuff or defeat,
You can lie there and cringe or whine,
Or come fighting, back to your feet!

I don't care if you're knocked down flat,
And life gives you the count of ten,
The big thing is, will you lie there?
Or get up! And fight on, again!

You say you're licked? You fool!
Defeat is a part of God's plan,
By which He tests if the stuff in you
Is fit to be called a man!

So, get up man! Get up on your feet!
Square off and forget that fall,
Even an angle worm, if cut in two,
Will keep right on trying to crawl!

Yes, there are two paths leading out,
From every retreat and rebuff.
But here's to the man who gets right up,
And calls old defeat's big bluff.

E. M. Johnson

Mariners

Each man must sail the sea of life
Mariners on earth are we.
From birth to death our course we sail,
From earth to eternity.

Our voyage on earth is brief
But a breath and we sail on our way.
Our passage we pay for one of two ports—
Darkness or the fair Port of Day.

There is no twilight harbor.
We sail after death toward night,
Or we sail despite the waves or the gale
To the Port of Eternal Light.

The Spectrum

Man sees Truth through a glass darkened,
Deep is the fog obscuring man's sight.
What little of knowledge each age has sifted,
Is but some scattered rays of light.

Broad is the spectrum, too vast for vision
Man sees but a slender arc.
And yet there's something impels him forward
Groping, hoping, through the dark.
Onward then, man must press forward
Truth's bugle has never blown "Retreat"'
Each ray of scattered light though splintered,
Helps make God's spectrum at last complete.

E. M. Johnson

The Full Circle of Truth

The arc of wisdom widens,
Vaster today, the sweep.
Farther into the fathomless darkness
Of Truth's vast and boundless deep,
Each ray of Light penetrates.

Though the candle may be dim,
Deep shadows darken the hall,
Slowly the arc closes the circle,
As each ray of Light does fall,
Revealing some second of Truth.

Somewhere, sometime, known but to God,
Creator of day and of night,
The arc shall encompass the circle
In a blazing glory of Light,
Somehow, sometime, known but to God.

Brew from the Cauldron of Hell

So this is the day of appeasement!
Coexistence, the hypnotic spell,
Directed by the devil and his cohorts,
With a plan that was hatched in Hell.
Voiced now by mealymouthed mobsters,
Skilled in the tricks of the game,
Who have changed now their outward tactics,
But the end-product always the same.

The foolish, the timid, now welcome
This sweet smelling, hybrid weed.
But men of wisdom always have known
Poison hemlock sprouts from hemlock seed.
You do not gather wheat from thistles.
The heart of a hybrid, hides always concealed
that which in the fullness of its cycle,
Shall surely, by time be revealed.

Be not deceived by this modern Janus,
Who now shows the smiling face!
The communist plan is to conquer man,
And enslave the human race.
Then rise, you men who fitfully slumber,
Break the chains of his hypnotic spell!
This sweet smelling essence, Coexistence,
Was brewed in the cauldrons of Hell!

E. M. Johnson

Worries, Stress and Strain

Too many, in these days of plenty,
In our frenzied struggle for wealth,
Forget as we strain for still greater gain,
To hoard the gold bonds of health.
Little can avail in life, if we fail,
To secure values of worth.
We leave all behind on the trails that wind,
To the uplands beyond the earth.

Who has found happiness in things,
In rings of the palace of kings?
What is gained in life if we find but strife,
And the turmoil wealth oft brings?
If what we gain brings naught but pain,
Worries, and strain and stress,
Far happier than the man at ease,
Though less he may possess.

Riches

There's something richer by far than gold,
There's something greater than fame;
There's something can neither be bought nor sold,
And that is a man's good name.

There's something greater than wealth by far,
There's that which is higher than creed,
There's something shines brighter than even a star,
And that is a kindly deed.

E. M. Johnson

Tempered Steel

Welcome the wind and challenge the storm
Face into the fiercest gales!
No skipper ever learned to handle his ship
By trimming in the harbor the sails.

No spruce tree or pine or mighty oak
Ever grew to a mast in a field.
No hero attained his soldier's fame
By marching on parade with shield.

No marathon run has ever been won
By playing golf in a country club.
No distance swimmer ever crossed the Channel
Who trained in a porcelain tub.

Then welcome the wind, the wave, the storm,
Hang on to that battered wheel!
The sword that's been heated red in the fire,
Is the blade with the tempered steel.

Philosophical Poems

A Projection into the Country Beyond

The following is merely my own
Projection into that vast mystery
Of the subconscious and its probable
Yes, possible direct connection
With the Universal Mind,
The Mind of God, that contains
Within itself, all wisdom that was
Before time began and was when
The span of space ran out
Its ever widening circle of creation,
Is now and ever shall be
When time has at last run
Its full course, to begin once again
Perhaps on still a wider circle
Of continued creation.

Here and there but always rare
Are a few minds that can
Temporarily lose all impressions
Of the objective mind and reaching out
Make direct contact with
The Universal Mind, that
Depository of all knowledge
That ever was, is or shall be.
Then from this contact bring up
Into the objective mind those
Impressions received from
The Universal Mind,
That Ancient of Ancients,
The Mind of God.

E. M. Johnson

Shoddy Cloth or a Garment of Gold?

The mind is the designer.
The act that follows is the outer garment
Woven in detail on the loom of the mind.
The outer is but the image,
The reflection of the inner.

We receive or send forth wave lengths at will
Ours the choice, for good, or ill.
And the garment that's woven for all to behold,
May be shoddy cloth, or a raiment pure gold.

Whatever, no matter what e're it may be
Thought is the thread.
The mind is the loom—
Its design is distorted, or bears an outline, divine.

Philosophical Poems

How Did You Meet Defeat?

It's not what happened yesterday,
Though bitter was defeat,
This is what counts in the sight of God—
How did you, disaster meet?

Did you cringe or cry or whimper,
Did self-pity bring the tear?
Were you filled with bitter hatred,
Your mind besieged by fear?

Or did you say, "Whate'er befalls,
God help me play the man!
I'll fit the broken bits together,
And try, Oh God, again!"

E. M. Johnson

The Loom

There is a pattern we weave each day
Upon the loom of life;
Some strands are those of joys we've known
Some threads are those of strife.
Yet weave we must, there is not choice,
For thus each life is wrought.
And the pattern woven day by day
Is shaped by each day's thought.

As stars set the patterns above us
In the night skies deep, dark blue
So, the design of all of our lives
Is set by the things we do.
Yet deeds are but outward expressions
Of the patterns woven within.
For deeds to thoughts are related
Closer than closest kin.

Think not to alter the future by
Weaving new strands tomorrow.
The present contains in itself
The future's joy or sorrow.
You blend of the loom of life
Bits of blue and of gray
But the cloth of the future is colored
By the strands woven today.

Philosophical Poems

Weave, we must, no matter how
We blend the strands of life.
Some strands of joy and some of sorrow
A blending of happiness and strife.
Slowly but surely the pattern shapes up
Strand upon strand is wrought;
For the warp and woof of every life
Is woven and shaped by thought.

E. M. Johnson

Harmonic

All round about us, like waves of the sea,
Ever encircling is God's harmony.
List to the whispering winds, in tune,
Gently rocking the new crescent moon.

There, on the hill top, hark to the morn,
Whose trumpet announces a new day is born.
Faint fairy cymbals echo from the glen,
The contralto of thrushes, the tenor of the wren.

Blue bells swing as they ring out their chimes,
Rivulets murmur their old runic rhymes.
All round about us, could we but hear,
Are the harmonies of God, so faint, yet so clear.

But the discords of life, mute the true notes,
We scarce hear the music that heavenward floats,
Swelling, then ebbing, like tides of the sea,
Striking the cords of God's harmony.

Philosophical Poems

An Ancient Wisdom

There's an ancient, ageless wisdom
That was old, when the hills were young.
I've sensed it as I roamed the woods
Where the Hang-Bird's nest is hung.

It's there on the hills, it's there in the rills
Or the life in the depths of the sea.
In the fearless flight of the "honkers" at night
I've sensed this hidden mystery.

I've seen it when some wild mother-hen
Has concealed the eggs in her nest.
I've seen it when alerted deer, stood,
Silhouetted 'neath a pine on a crest.

I've seen it in the maneuvering swallows
Teaching their young to wheel.
It's there, in the star flower's symmetry
And the stamp of the solomon seal.

But seek no Rosetta Stone on earth
To unlock this age-old mystery.
The key to this ageless Wisdom
Must be sought in the sands of Eternity.

E. M. Johnson

The Mystery

Some reason by an evolving process,
Came Earth, the Stars and Man.
From simple to complex, runs their circle.
And they end just where they began,
In the quest of the mystery of creation.

But evolution is not the full answer,
Though it may, give many men glory,
The vision of man can only scan
A few pages of the full story,
In the compendium of creation.

Deeply imprinted and coiled in the cell,
And deep in the atom's heart,
God has hidden a Plan that unfolds,
And grows to an integral part,
Of the endless intricate Design of Creation.

Time is naught in God's progression,
Slowly the scroll unrolls.
From Light to matter, from Amoeba to man,
The Wisdom of God unfolds.
In the timeless aeons from stardust to sod
The mystery of it all, is known but to God.
Or yet, in the womb of Time.

Inherent in light is matter.
But hidden in matter, is life.
Which throughout endless time
Has unfolded with the changing epochs

Into life, as we know it today.
And the imprint of all that was,
Or the imprint of all that is,
And whatever of life yet shall be
Was hidden by God in the atoms
Of the galaxies, the sun and the sea.

The crowning of God's evolving process
Was the unfoldment of Life in man,
Made in the image of his Creator
But man is more than matter
Since God is more than energy.
God is spirit, the whole, the part
As he breathed into man, into every heart
Something of Himself, that must return
Back to the ultimate source
Back to God, the beginning
Back to God, the part, and the whole
For God is the End, and the Final Goal.

E. M. Johnson

Then Cherish Beauty

Memories of beauty stored in the heart
Sunset or flower or tree,
Or a slow, flowing sibilant stream
The wild breaking waves of the sea
Will orient the soul as it seeks its goal
And fill the heart with a leaven
Revealing in the darkness of earth
Some dim, faint flush of heaven.

Miss not nor mar the mystic charm
Surrounding us, one and all.
There's treasure that nothing can measure
In a crumbling lichened wall.
There's beauty beneath life's sordidness
Could we but clearly see;
There's the imprint in all things 'round us,
The stamp of divinity.

Then, store all beauty deep in the heart
Miss not a thing on your way.
For life is brief, it is but a breath
From birth to the end of your day.
The memories of beauty, whatever they be
Sunset or flowers that nod,
Each bit of beauty stored in the heart
Brings us closer to God.

Philosophical Poems

From Dawn Unto Darkness

Dawn and the flight of darkness
And over the mountain wall
God in the shafts of sunlight;
Duty's incessant call.

Noontide and the welcome shadows,
Respite from desk and plow;
Sunshine pouring now earthward
To the heart of bush and bough.

Sunset and Angelus hour,
Deep in the gold of the west;
Memory's tear drop incense
Distilled deep in the breast.

Twilight and far in the darkness,
As the stars drift back to the sky,
The throbbing night wind's whisper
Is answered by the night bird's cry.

E. M. Johnson

Polarization

When the compass of the soul
Is magnetized by pleasure,
The needle will then, no longer swing
True, toward the heart's rich treasure.

When the fragile strings of the heart,
Are discorded by earthbound things,
No overtones of life then, rise and
Heavenward float on fairy wings.

When the higher centers of the mind, are
Short-circuited by self and greed,
No longer then, will the heart be stirred
By some brother's distress and need.

For the soul, the heart and the mind,
Can but one master serve!
The inviolate law of life is this:
Toward thy treasure, thou must swerve!

Lightly Time Steals O'er the Heart

How strange that hearts once crushed with pain
By life so torn to shred,
Time with it's magic heals again
And dries the tears once shed.
The wounds of life with hurt so deep,
They seared the very soul,
Time somehow with its healing warmth
Can once again make whole.

Like winds that whisper to the waves
Across some woodland gem,
Or like the throb of early morn
As dawn burns night's dark hem,
Thus softly time steals 'cross the heart
And tissues over pain,
Till memory probes deep in the wound
To break the heart again.

E. M. Johnson

Beyond Recall

No more can you recall the word
That pained a brother's heart,
Than you can set back into place
Rose petals that you've plucked apart.

No more can you bring back again
The scenes of yesterday,
Than you call back the zephyrs
That have passed you on their way.

How can you mend a friendship,
Whose fragile wings you've torn
Than you can steal the jewels from
The dews of early morn.

Beyond recall is each harsh word
As the wandering winds of the west,
Can the light of a love that has gently dimmed
Burn brightly again in the breast?

Philosophical Poems

These Alone Can Man Possess

The only wealth you'll e'er possess
Of all your earthbound gain,
The only treasures of this world
You clutch and still retain,
Are found in beauty and in love,
In friends or kindness done,
The love of God and your fellowman,
Or the glory of the gold in the sun.

Then cherish these and claim them all,
These riches from on high.
For love and friendship are eternal,
They tarnish not, they never die.
Of all earth's treasures, these alone,
You take, when you depart.
Earth repossesses whatever does not
Enrich the human heart.

E. M. Johnson

The Fourth Dimension

Each hill now humpbacked by old age,
Conceals beneath its rain-scarred brow,
The span called time, which once has been,
That which shall be, is ever now.

Each drop of rain from ocean's breast,
That rides the clouds on high,
Contains within its ceaseless cycle,
The measureless aeons of the sky.

Each moment of our lives, though brief
Contains all time that e'er shall be.
Within each moment there lies concealed,
Time, the unsolved mystery.

Philosophical Poems

Treasure Beyond Measure

There is wealth beneath the sea,
There's a wealth found deep in mines,
But it shines not with the luster
Of the gold that love refines.

There are jewels of the earth,
There are fortunes hid in clay;
Yet no treasure can compare
With the gold at break of day.

There is a music of the artist,
Rich with purest harmony;
This is discord when compared
With the e'en tide's symphony.

There is power in the stream,
That man's genius now has caught;
Yet it dwarfs when it's compared
With the hidden force of thought.

All the beauty, and all the wealth
That on earth we e'er can find,
Cannot compare with that treasure
God has stored in the mind.

For the best that man attempts
E'er he sinks back to the sod,
Be it work of plow or pen,
Is to think the thoughts of God.

Yes there's wealth beneath the seas,
There's the treasure of the mind;
But the richest wealth of the earth
Is a thought that is divine.

E. M. Johnson

Contentment

Some seek success and happiness,
And wealth and friends and fame;
Thinking it thus, man does gain
An abiding Granite-name.

It makes me think of Him who said,
Who builds his house on sand
Will find it tumbled into ruin,
When the winds blow o'er the land.

There is no doubt some wealth and gain
And structures fine we need,
But I wonder if cathedrals great
Do not fossilize our creed?

IT seems to me that greater barns
And houses rich and fine
Shut out the glory of the sun,
Blot out the stars that shine!

Somehow the fences and the walls
That set great halls apart
Oft set the mortar and sift the sand
Around the owner's heart.

I used to wonder why the Teacher great
Chose fishermen from the sea,
But now I've learned just why he did
Choose men from Galilee.

Philosophical Poems

He knew that wealth, if made an end,
That rank and power of peers,
Does oftimes cramp and warp the soul
And dries the well of tears.

No I'm content to plod along
And live close to the sod.
For though I may miss wealth and fame,
I'll still see bluebells nod!

Yes, I'm content to pass up wealth,
And stay close to the sod;
Seems somehow easier for common folks
To live a bit closer to God.

So you men of wealth, who worry about health,
Who feel that things bring joy,
I'll wager the moon 'gainst your silver spoon
My happiness has less alloy!

No, keep your worries and market flurries,
Just let me plod along;
For when your discords smite you deaf,
I'll still be hearing a song!

My roses will bloom and shed perfume
Straight to the soul of me,
The open sky and the lone bird's cry,
And the wind in my Norway tree!

No, I'm content to have heaps less
Of things that rubbish the mind;

E. M. Johnson

I'd trade them all, both fame and hall,
For a heart that's ever kind.

Just the open mind and a spirit free,
And the will to do and dare;
Just a friend or two, some work to do,
 And at twilight, rest and prayer.

So keep your walls, your stocks, your halls
You fellows who struggle for fame;
Just give me the sod where bluebells nod,
And God is more than a name!

Philosophical Poems

The Quest

I met a man in search of happiness.
He had sought for years, in vain.
His heart was as empty as the summer cloud
That drifts away, without rain.

I met a man, who never sought happiness,
Yet his heart was filled with treasure.
For he poured into life from the springs of his soul
Cheer and love, without measure.

Yes search if you will, over vale, over hill,
Or roam the world, so wide,
But never will happiness brim your heart
If greed or self, there abide.

E. M. Johnson

High Through the Heavens

Wider than the sky and higher than the star,
Knowledge stretches out and beyond there, afar,
Slowly but surely there's more light in the dark,
As science inevitably increases man's arc.
Propelled by an urge, man seeks day and night,
To dispel some shadow, let in some bit of light.

Endless still and endless,
the how, the when and the why,
Each answer but a step, on the stairway to the sky.
Hopeless oft the queries seem, God's wisdom is so vast,
Our very life so brief, but a breath and all is past.
Time, the endless current, carries on the human race,
Truth, the expanding circle is rimmed about by space.

Each bit of knowledge, but a grain of sand,
Flung across eternity, by God's great hand,
To be gathered again together, in one fell sweep,
When He reshapes the heavens,
The earth and the ocean's deep.
Yet man must ever gather, gather while he may,
The impelling urge for knowledge,
Proving him more than clay.

Man the self-blinded spirit, stumbles on in the night,
Knowledge is the pathway, truth the morning light.
God is the fountain from which the rivulets course,
Spreading out forever, yet returning to the source.
Onward still and endless, stretching out after,
High though the heavens, beyond each star, a star.

Philosophical Poems

A Bit of Contrast

I wonder how much we'd cherish the sun
If there were no clouds or rain?
I wonder how much we'd know the joy
If we'd never known some pain?

I wonder how much we'd strive for the right
Had we never through failure known wrong?
I wonder how much we'd shun the discords
IF we'd never known strains of sweet song?

I wonder how hard we'd strive for success
If failure were part of God's plan?
I wonder how much we'd know of Truth,
If Christ had not come as a man?

I wonder how much we'd welcome the spring
If winter prevailed through the year?
I wonder how much we'd know of laughter
If we'd never known a tear?

For life seems a blending of sorrow and joy,
Of shadow and most of light
And somehow by contrast we come to know
That God made these things just right.

E. M. Johnson

Cause and Effect

What may seem more coincidence,
Or just a happenstance,
Perhaps may have a deeper cause,
Than just the law of chance.

If all things are related, and
From cause must come effect,
To call events coincidence,
Is reasoning, with defect.

There's nothing in this world alone,
The winds foretell the weather.
And all events no matter what,
Are all bound up together.

Full Runs the Spring

There is a well where much when drawn
Has ever more to offer;
There is a treasure when given away
Refills the empty coffer.
There is a light when shared with others
Who stumble in the dark,
Grows ever brighter in the night,
Though it seemed at first a spark.

Every heart when drained which shares
Something with some other,
That offers all it may possess,
To ease some burdened brother,
Refills itself in some strange way
From a source in springs above;
For the wells of the heart run never dry,
If the water withdrawn is love.

E. M. Johnson

Liberalism

To be liberal, then
Is to be broad-minded!
So broad, in fact
That you look at all things,
And see nothing,
In its entirety.
To swallow all things,
And digest nothing,
That can be assimilated
By the mind and the spirit.

To believe all things,
Hence nothing,
That can motivate
The will to action,
For a better life.
To accept all, because it's new

For the old is nothing,
But to be cast aside,
As a worn-out garment,
Forgetting that in the new,
Is always some of the old.

No, if to be liberal means
To broaden the vision,
Of the mind
So we can see all things
To all people,

Philosophical Poems

And stand for all things,
Thus stand for nothing,
That is eternal and true
Then thank God
Some of us are narrow
And some of us are blind!

E. M. Johnson

An Ancient Law

There are two sides to the coin of living.
The one is stamped "getting" the other is "giving".
The one is the compliment of the other.
But how often the side of "giving" we cover,
Each time we do, something in the heart we smother.

True living, then, is giving from the heart's full treasure
Pressed down, overflowing the fullest measure.

If this we do, we shall learn how true
Is this ancient Law of ancient ways,
"That to him who gives, God fills his days
With plenty and to spare."

What Did He Bring Back Home?

Now this man had wealth but not much else
So he too, took his trip abroad.
He traveled in style down the old river Nile
Through Greece to Paris and Rome—
Then bored with it all he flew back home.

What did he bring back, you ask me?
Well, little he'd brought, so it was but naught
That he carried with him back home.
None of the grandeur that once was Rome
None of the beauty of Grecian thought
Or the marvels of sculpture her artists wrought.
No nothing but things, baubles and rings
But nothing that fills the heart so full it sings
And renders humble thanks unto Him
Who shapes the destiny of emperors or kings.

Where our treasure is, that is the heart's true measure.
Back with us is brought whatever we sought—
No matter where we may roam, we bring back home
The beauty we brought with us, to Greece or Rome.

E. M. Johnson

Nature Abhors A Vacuum

Where there is hope, there cannot be doubt,
Where there is faith, there is no fear.
Where there is love, there cannot be hate,
And evil is routed, when God draws near.

Where there is light, there is no darkness,
Where there is freedom, slavery had sped.
Where there is vision, leading a nation,
Bondage is chained and tyranny dead.

Where there is courage, cowardice is ambushed,
Where there is character, weakness unknown.
Where there is charity and human kindness,
There you will find a soul full grown.

Continuity

There's a oneness in Creation,
In the flower and star on high;
There's a harmony and relation
In all things of earth and sky.

The Law that brims the tear drop,
Is the Law that builds the star;
Tis the Law that sends the rain drop
To the ocean's rim so far.

Tis the Law that moves a mountain,
Builds future crags beneath the sea;
And the Law fills every fountain,
Shapes the worlds that yet shall be.

That same Law leads man apace,
Ever upward toward his goal;
That same Law spans rimless space,
Guides man's inner spirit-born soul.

There's a oneness in Creation—
All are thoughts of God's own mind;
There's a oneness and interrelation
Deep in the hearts of all man kind.

E. M. Johnson

Universality

There is but one law—that law is God.
But God is love.
And all things that are, have been or shall be,
The stars in the heavens, the isles in the sea,
All mass and motion here or above—
In the final analysis, of star or of sod,
The precipitate of all is the eternal God.

Philosophical Poems

Giants of the Earth

Circumstance ne'er made a man
Of great repute or fame,
Nor family tree or high or low
Create a granite name.

Nor do I hold that school can weld
Or mold the truest worth;
There's more intangible
Creates the giants of earth.

Coordination of the heart
And of the hand and mind,
Then blend with this a vision clear,
And love for all mankind.

Ah, then you have Damascus steel
That cuts the Gordian knot;
Of this I hold are born the great,
Who cannot be forgot.

E. M. Johnson

Greater Than Thebes or Rome

I searched the record of ancient script
And toiled through their musty pages,
Hoping to find the one Law of Truth
In the Scroll of the Scribes and Sages.

I felt could I find but the Law Universal
The key to all knowledge I'd know,
A sesame I'd find would open the mind
To the fullness of life here below.

So I toiled through the ruins of Babylon
Through the pages of ancient Greece
But naught could I find would give my mind
From that burning desire surcease.

Then I sailed cross the bay to old Pompey
And searched 'mid the dust of Rome.
Yet naught did I see, to enlighten me,
Though I searched through tome after tome.

Weary in mind and foot sore and spent
I returned to my own cottage door,
And despite the laboring years of toil
No wiser was I than before.

For the musty pages of ancient script,
Though enriched with the gold of sages,
Had failed to teach me what there I sought,
The one Great Law of the ages.

Philosophical Poems

No open sesame to knowledge I'd found,
The key to Truth did I see,
In Thebes or Rome nor the sun baked tome
Of Babylon or old Chaldes.

But seated one day beneath an old pine
That leaned o'er my cabin home,
I found in a flower, the trees and a shower
What I sought for in Thebes and Rome.

E. M. Johnson

Sands on the Sea Shore

As mass is made of molecule,
And these of atoms small,
And atoms made of particles,
That cannot be seen at all,
Thus truth is made of laws,
And these of facts men found,
In nature and in those events,
That do all life surround.

We smash the atom into energy,
And energy back to mass.
We've learned this awesome awful truth,
For man's destruction also.
We've learned the law, but not the truth,
That knowledge is for peace.
Unless we come to know this well,
Our troubles shall not cease.

We gather slowly grain by grain,
On truth's endless shore,
But as we gather, then we learn
There's more and more and more.
Hopeless as this seems to be,
And all or efforts vain,
Yet man, by God, has been impelled,
To gather grain by grain.

Perchance in some dim distant time,
Truth's fullness man shall know,
And then in peace all men shall dwell

Philosophical Poems

In brotherhood, here below.
Or must this come when time shall end,
When earth shall be no more,
And God has gathered to himself,
The sands of the endless shore.

E. M. Johnson

Higher Than Creed

Someone planted a fruit tree seed
Near a dusty, winding road,
And long years after, beneath its shade
A traveler unstrapped his heavy load.

Someone spoke a kindly word
To a stranger foot sore and weary,
And somehow the gloom and clouds so gray
Grew bright and the world grew cheery.

Someone lifted a helping hand
To a stranger stumbling in the mire,
And strength flowed into that helping hand
That lifted the stranger and helper higher.

Someone had a kindly thought,
And passed it on to a friend.
It grew like the tree and shed perfume
From heart to heart without end.

For the thought and the word and the helping hand
And the shade that grew from that seed
Reveal in their growth a law divine,
Higher than man-made creed.

Kinship

I believe I am a part of everything,
And everything is a part of me.
If God is the Father of all creation,
Then how else could anything be?

Man came from God as an Entity of Thought,
An embryonic replica of divinity.
With inherent propulsion to grow to God's likeness,
In the fullness of Time in Eternity.

For all that is in the earth or sky,
Planet or man, or flower or tree,
All and everything from the beginning,
Came from, and returns to, the Source of Energy.

E. M. Johnson

Could it be Something Intangible?

What then is the eternal,
That which is the greater worth?
Is it found in what we clutch and touch,
And all such matters of earth?
If not, then why this constant striving,
To attain renown or fame,
To amass great wealth or power,
Or win a worthy name?

Do these bring the heart contentment,
The peace of mind and soul?
Are these the worthwhile things,
That we have set as our goal?
If not, what then is, the Eternal
That we should seek to find?
Could it, do you think, be something intangible,
Found in the heart, the soul, the mind?

Philosophical Poems

Riding the Storm

Unless you've braved both wind and wave
In life's full tidal conflict,
By the winds of fate, you'll be driven adrift,
And grounded, a worthless derelict.

Rudderless then with mast aslant,
And torn to shreds your sail,
What hope have you to reach the port
In life's lashing, withering gale?

Unless you've battled through storms of life
And fought its winds and sleet
You've little chance to miss the reefs
And the shoals of utter defeat.

Then, welcome the winds and the blasting blow
That sweep o'er the seas of life.
No skipper ever anchored safe in a port
Who had never faced storm or strife.

E. M. Johnson

A Path across a Hill

There is a path, I've sometimes walked,
That leads across a hill,
Beyond which lies a valley,
Where all is calm and still.
The path is blazed, I know that well,
Yet, I have missed it oft.
With eyes that looked, but failed to read,
The signs raised there, aloft.

So often, when I've wandered far,
Seemed lost in doubts and fear,
I've turned and found the path I sought,
Was right beside me here;
And when my feet had found the path,
My doubts and fears were gone.
No longer was I burdened for
My heart was filled with song.

I don't know why I miss the signs,
So plainly marked are all.
I only know each time I do,
I stumble and I fall.
There is a Guide who knows this path,
No man has walked alone;
If I would only follow Him,
What joys would be my own.

The hill we climb you see, is Life,
The valley stretching far
That Land we hope to reach some day,

Philosophical Poems

Beyond the farthest star.
The wilderness, we roam, is where
We wander from God's sight.
The blaze-marks on the path are His,
The Guide, The Lord, The Light!

E. M. Johnson

Forever Cycling

Eternally God molds matter from energy
Then resolves it back into light.
For change is a law of the universe
Though often concealed from sight.

There is nothing static in creation
Nor mountains, nor plains or sea.
For change is the only permanence which
Cycling, wheels on toward infinity.

Every tree or flower, every drop in a shower
Every star or planet in its course
Reveals this cycling change of creation
Proving thereby, its ultimate source.

There is nothing permanent, save change.
What is static, cannot remain.
For God is not a God of permanence
What He's molded, He will remold again.

All life on earth must yield to this Law
Which is above, the decrees of man.
For God, by this law of change universal
Reshapes all matter according to Plan.

Philosophical Poems

Chinks in the Wall

Let no man think to build a wall,
And every chink to fill,
Around his soul, though resolute,
With the mortar of his will.
No matter what the mixture be,
Or heredity stirred therein,
The corrosive fingers of evil in time,
Will somehow probe within.

And once the entrance then is gained,
The will dulled full asleep,
Across the rimmed ramparts, then
The hosts of evil sweep.
Each broken block of resolutions,
Set carefully against all strain,
Shall fall apart in every heart,
For the will alone, is vain.

There is but one ingredient known,
If mixed with the lime and sand,
Can every corrosive action of evil,
Each weakening blast, withstand.
By some, it is called the Spirit of God,
But the name, does it matter after all?
It is Love alone can cement every stone,
In the soul's susceptible wall.

E. M. Johnson

The Gleam

As I study my volumes of history,
And ponder their printed pages,
I catch the glow of a gleam, whose rays
Grow brighter, down through the ages.

I note the long stretches of darkness,
When the gleam was burning low,
Yet deep in the hearts of mankind,
God kept that gleam aglow.

Safe from the storms of selfishness,
Safe from the gale of greed,
God kept that light burning in the night,
As He hides each plant in its seed.

Though empires may cast their shadows,
And dim for an age, the beam,
The breath of God shall rekindle,
Each flickering ray of that gleam.

For He who can level yon mountain,
And sift its dust 'neath the sea,
Will crush both empire and ruler, that
Trims not the lamp of liberty.

So I fear neither storms, nor the darkness,
Nor the shadows of dictators and might;
I know that God will preserve the glow,
Of the gleam of justice and right!

Philosophical Poems

So Little, Yet So Great

There's a little word too seldom heard,
In these days of rare restraint.
And yet it's the key to the character,
Of every sinner or saint.

It takes up the slack in a spineless back,
And sparks the spirit to aspire,
To climb the heights and shun the delights,
Of selfish human desire.

This word that is heard so seldom,
In a world of worry and woe,
Is the little simple, two lettered word
The character builder, "No!"

E. M. Johnson

Triumphant

Out of the depths that surround me,
    surging, o'erwhelming my soul;
Faint through the ink stained midnight
    Flickers a light o'er the shoal.

Faint, yet clear shines the Beacon,
    Piercing the ominous dark
Guiding a storm tossed mariner,
    Alone in a storm tossed bark.

Loud roar the breakers around me,
    Salt waves blot out the dim star;
And clear o'er the tempest that rages
    The breakers leap over the bar.

Yet despite the gloom and the darkness,
    Spite of the roar of the gale,
A voice from the heart's inner chamber
    Whispers, "Thy soul, cannot fail!"

So I lift my eyes to that Beacon,
    And set the rudder of my soul;
For the light that shines at the midnight,
    Will guide me safe toward my goal.

Though my main sail be torn to tatters,
    And splintered, the mizzen mast head,
I'll sail toward that light that beckons,
    While the waves are preparing my bed.

Philosophical Poems

I may go down neath the billows,
    To a resting place, deep and still;
But the rudder of my heart shall be pointing
    Straight toward that Light on the hill.

Then out of the depths that surge o'er me,
    My soul yet triumphant, shall rise;
And sail toward that unchanged ocean
    That lies far beyond the blue skies.

E. M. Johnson

Mister Big

And so he enlarged his factory,
This man of vision, so rare.
Carefully laying his plans to build
Where lesser men never would dare.
And he crushed all smaller units,
That blocked his upward path,
Nor cared, in his ruthless manner,
What followed as aftermath.

Was he his brother's keeper?
Let others strive and strain.
His one ambition, to build and build,
And pile each gain upon gain.
Profit, this was the countersign,
Greater each plant must be.
Forgetting that bigness means nothing,
In the street called Eternity.

But the world bowed to his greatness,
Weak men grovelled at his feet,
This captain of industry, grown mighty,
Who would never accept defeat.
"Am I my brother's keeper?
I've striven with main and might,
And what I've gained, I've worked for,
Yes, struggled, both day and night."

And the world hailed his greatness,
They lauded and they cheered,
Forgetting, in their blindness, those

Philosophical Poems

Whose souls this man had seared.
Profit, profit, his password,
Greater each plant built he,
Heedless that his greatness was nothing,
On the street called Eternity.

"Am I my brother's keeper?
What I've built, I've built alone!"
So he built him a greater mansion,
The finest ever made of stone.
And he walled himself there securely,
While he ruled o'er men, called free,
Forgetting his fullness was mere emptiness,
In the street called Eternity.

For the needle's eye is small,
Which leads to that eternal street.
Far too small, I fear, for those who
Crush their brothers beneath their feet.
Are we our brother's keeper?
Does any man build alone?
Perhaps this man will find the answer,
When he faces the Judgement Throne.

E. M. Johnson

Three Men and a Mountain

Three men stood viewing a mountain
In the glowing glory of twilight,
Watching the sunset now raising
The far flung banner of night.

"It would be quite a job," said the first,
"But I know it could be done:
I'd build my road around that shoulder,
Then straight toward the setting sun."

"Look at those trees," said the second,
"An owner of a large lumber mill,
I'd build a sluice and I'd slide my logs,
Straight down the side of that hill."

The third man, somber and silent,
Filled with a glow by the glory,
Beheld in the mountain twilight,
Scenes for a poem or a story.

Each man viewing the mountain,
This handiwork of God's design,
Each man took from the mountain
Just what he brought to this shrine.

Philosophical Poems

Linnaea Borealis

I know a secret, fairy nook,
Beside a meandering, murmuring brook;
Where angels, ages ago once trod,
As glad they did, a task that God
Had bid them do.

Dark cedar trees, may there be found,
And on the damp moss covered ground,
Linnaea Borealis, the Twin Flower fair,
Pours from her heart an incense rare,
Upon the breeze.

For deep within that secret nook,
Beside the meandering, murmuring brook;
The angels knelt on that moss covered sod,
And planted, ages ago, some Thoughts of God
For me and you.

E. M. Johnson

The Body, the Mind, the Soul

"What then is life?" the teacher asked
Of scholars who sat by his side,
As he sought to teach them the truth
And error to brush aside.

Then up spoke one, of jovial mien,
That life was made for pleasure.
That man should live in the physical,
And drink its depths without measure.

Then spoke the man who was deep in thought,
Who sat as one in a dream.
"In the realm of the mind alone, is Life,
The mind alone, is supreme."

Soft spoke the next with head bowed low,
"Man's life is found in the soul.
Torture the body, lift up the soul!
This alone should be our goal."

Then spoke the teacher: "Learn now the truth,
Only part of living, you see.
Life is the body, mind and the soul,
The fullness of life is all three."

Come, on Fairy Wings

Oh, fleeting muse, who knows my needs,
Tune now my muted strings,
Softly breathe o'er the broken reeds.
And give some thought, its wings.

Just give me one short lay,
One thought to cheer some soul,
Lonely, groping its winding way,
Seeking some glimmering goal.

Then come, Oh muse, on fairy wings,
Need you tarry so long?
Draw the bow lightly over the strings,
Oh grant but one sweet song.

E. M. Johnson

Epilogue

If I could have caught just one short phrase
From God's great realm of thought
And know that to some lonely heart
One word of hope I'd brought,
I would not have lived in vain.

If I could have staked the boundaries of
One thought, or e'en its arc,
To loom, a blaze, on life's dim path
For someone, stumbling in the dark.
I would not have lived in vain.

Tis this impels me e'er to try,
In hope, that as I write,
Some spark of mine may set aglow
A candle, shining in the night,
If so, perchance, I've not then lived in vain.

To order additional copies of

Philosophical Poems

or receive a copy of the complete
Savage Press catalog,

contact us at:

Phone Orders: 1-800-732-3867

Voice and Fax: (715) 394-9513

e-mail: savpress@spacestar.com

Visit online at: www.savpress.com

Visa or MasterCard accepted

Box 115, Superior, WI 54880 (715) 394-9513

Other Savage Press Books Available

Poetry

In the Heart of the Forest by Diana Randolph
Appalachian Mettle by Paul Bennett
Treasures from the Beginning of the World by Jeff Lewis
Gleanings from the Hillsides by E.M. Johnson
Thicker Than Water by Hazel Sangster
Mystic Bread by Mike Savage
Moments Beautiful Moments Bright by Brett Bartholomaus
Pathways by Mary B. Wadzinski
Treasured Thoughts by Sierra

Fiction

The Year of the Buffalo, a novel of love and minor league baseball
by Marshall J. Cook
Something in the Water by Mike Savage
Burn Baby Burn by Mike Savage
Voices from the North Edge by St. Croix Writers
Keeper of the Town by Don Cameron
The Lost Locomotive of the Battle-Axe by Mike Savage

Nonfiction

Business

SoundBites by Kathy Kerchner
Dare to Kiss the Frog by van Hauen, Kastberg & Soden

Sports and Travel

Sailboat Log Book by Don Handy, Illus. by Gordon Slotness
Canoe & Kayaker's Floating Log Book by Don Handy
The Duluth Tour Book & the North Shore Tour Book
by Jeff Cornelius

Essay, Humor, Reminiscence

Hometown Wisconsin by Marshall J. Cook
Jackpine Savages by Frank Larson
The Heart's Journey Home by Jill Downs
Widow of the Waves by Bev Jamison

Local & Regional History

Stop in the Name of the Law by Alex O'Kash
Beyond the Mine by Peter J. Benzoni
Some Things You Never Forget by Clem Miller
Superior Catholics by Cheney and Meronek